THE MATT MERTON
MYSTERIES

THE END: PART 1

Paul Blum

RISING ★ STARS

nasen

NASEN House, 4/5 Amber Business Village, Amber Close,
Amington, Tamworth, Staffordshire B77 4RP

Rising Stars UK Ltd.
22 Grafton Street, London W1S 4EX
www.risingstars-uk.com

Text © Rising Stars UK Ltd.
The right of Paul Blum to be identified as the author of this work has
been asserted by him in accordance with the Copyright, Design and
Patents Act, 1988.

Published 2010

Cover design: pentacorbig
Illustrator: Chris King, Illustration Ltd
Photos: Alamy
Text design and typesetting: pentacorbig/Clive Sutherland
Publisher: Gill Budgell
Editorial consultants: Lorraine Petersen and Dee Reid

British Library Cataloguing in Publication Data.
A CIP record for this book is available from the British Library.

ISBN: 978-1-84680-800-5

Printed by Craft Print International Limited, Singapore

THE MATT MERTON
MYSTERIES

CONTENTS

THE CRASH

The Crash happened in 2021. Alien
spaceships crash-landed on Earth.
Now the aliens rule the world. They
have changed shape so they look
like people. People call the aliens The
Enemy. Since The Crash, people are
afraid. They don't know who is an
Enemy and who is a friend.

An organisation called The Firm keeps
order on the streets. The Firm keeps
people safe from Enemy attacks — or
do they?

People are going missing and the Earth
is becoming colder and darker all the
time. A new ice age is coming ...

ABOUT MATT MERTON

Matt Merton works for The Firm. He often works with **Dexter**. Their job is to find and kill The Enemy. They use Truth Sticks to do this.

But Matt has problems. He has lost some of his memory and cannot answer some big questions.

Where has **Jane**, his girlfriend, gone?

How did he get his job with **The Firm**?

Matt thinks The Firm is on the side of good. But he is not sure ...

CHAPTER 1

Matt Merton sat in a cafe next to Jane and Sam. It was not Sam's cafe. The Firm had burnt his cafe down the night before.

'What are you drinking, Matt?' said Sam. Then he remembered. He would not be making his friend a drink today. The memory of what had happened the night before made poor Sam shake.

'Don't worry,' said Jane. 'I'll get the drinks.'

'Coffee, please Jane,' said Matt. 'Extra hot with an extra shot. For both of us.'

Matt put his hand on Sam's shoulder. Matt thought about the night before. He and Sam had been waiting in Sam's cafe for Jane. She and Matt were taking Sam with them to escape from The Firm. Someone blocked the cafe door. Then they set fire to it. Matt and Sam were trapped inside!

Jane got there just in time. She broke down the door and pulled them to safety. They drove through the night to a small town. They all knew it was The Firm who had tried to kill them.

Matt had worked for The Firm. But now Matt was on the run from them. He knew too much about their plans.

He had found out The Firm were working for the aliens and that meant killing humans. Anyone who had fought back against the real enemy went missing or was dead. At last, Matt knew who the real enemy was.

They were going to take over the world. But Jane had a plan to stop them.

Matt looked around the little cafe. 'Are we safe here?' he said.

'Yes, my friend runs this cafe,' said Jane. 'It's okay.'

Sam looked around. He was still scared. The fire and their escape had happened so fast. Matt drank his coffee and kept his head down.

Just then two men walked into the cafe. Jane tapped Matt on the arm. 'Those are the men who burnt down Sam's cafe last night,' she said. 'We need to go.'

The two men went up to the counter. They held up Matt's photo.

'We're from The Firm,' said the one with the dark glasses. 'Have you seen this man?'

'He likes his coffee hot, with an extra shot,' said the tall man.

Jane's friend was calm. 'I haven't seen him,' he said. 'But I will let you know if he ever stops by.'

The tall man leaned over the counter. He grabbed Jane's friend. 'You do that,' he said, 'or you'll be looking into my Truth Stick for so long you'll need new eyes!'

Matt, Jane and Sam had seen enough. They ran out of the back door and got into Jane's car.

'That was too close,' said Jane. 'You have to know the whole truth now.'

'The whole truth about what?' asked Sam.

'The truth about why I ran away on the night of The Crash,' she said. 'The truth about who we are really fighting and why. It's best for you to see it with your own eyes. Then I'll explain.'

Matt felt nervous. He could feel his heart thumping and his hands going sweaty. He had wanted Jane to come back for such a long time. He had sat in the shadows thinking about her for hours. He thought he would save her, but she had saved him. Now at last the gaps in his memory would be filled.

CHAPTER 2

Jane drove into the woods. She stopped the car under some trees.

The sky was dark. Since The Crash, it was always winter and never summer. Since The Crash, it snowed every day.

'It's colder than ever this morning,' said Matt. They shivered as they got out of the car to follow Jane into the woods.

Jane pointed up at the sky. 'There is a reason why it's so cold. What can you see?' They all looked up.

'It's so dark,' said Matt. 'It never used to be as dark as this during the day. There's no Sun.'

'You can't see that when you are in the city.'

'That's right,' said Jane. 'Since The Crash, The
Firm have been building a shield.

The shield stops the Sun's rays reaching Earth.
The aliens are making the Earth colder and darker
every day.'

'But why?' said Sam.

'The aliens come from a very cold planet,' Jane explained. 'They can only live in the cold. So our planet has to change to meet their needs.'

Sam got angry. 'So we will all die, so they can live,' he shouted.

Jane nodded. 'That's their plan.'

'And The Firm are helping them,' said Matt in a low voice. 'They are killing the old and the weak.'

'Matt, did you know about this?' asked Sam.

'Not the whole time. I was under their control. I was given drugs to take away my memory. Now I know the truth. I know they are the real enemy,' said Matt.

Jane nodded again. 'Matt not knowing the truth kept him alive. The Firm knew he would never stop trying to find me. They want me dead. On the night of The Crash there was so much confusion. I thought Matt was dead, so I ran.

From my hiding place I heard the alien leader giving orders. I knew they wanted to take over Earth. I found more survivors. We became an army who wanted to fight the aliens. The Firm called us The Enemy.'

Matt understood the truth at last. Suddenly, he felt very happy. He could change things. He could make things right.

'How can the three of us stop them?' said Matt.
'There are so many of them.'

'And there are more of us than you think,' she
said.

CHAPTER 3

'The aliens cannot find and kill all of us. Look at this map.' Jane's map showed a place called Route 6.

'I know about Route 6,' Matt said. 'It is a top secret and a very bad place.'

'What do you know?' asked Jane.

'A long time ago, I saw people being taken there on lorries,' said Matt. 'There were bars on all the windows. They were scared and could not escape.'

'Route 6 is where The Firm takes people who fight against them. These prisoners are drugged like you were, Matt. Then they work to keep the shield up. It takes a lot of power to make a new ice age happen,' said Jane.

'How do they do that?' said Matt.

'A computer keeps the shield in place above the Earth. The shield tracks the Sun's rays so that it can block them out. From when it rises in the east and sets in the west, the Sun is kept in the shadows,' Jane explained.

'So what happens if the shield comes down?' asked Sam.

The aliens will die from the heat and light. We'll be free. But we must get inside the main computer room at Route 6,' said Jane. 'We must destroy the computer and kill the alien leader. It's the only way.'

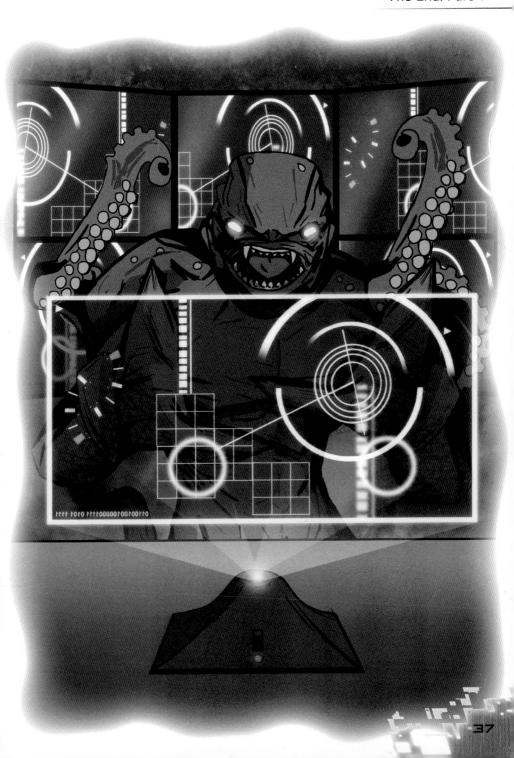

'Then it will be over. We'll have our lives back,' said Matt.

Jane nodded. 'But getting in there won't be easy. The aliens watch over Route 6. As the Earth gets colder, more of them arrive there. It will be very dangerous but the prisoners will help us.'

'How?' asked Sam. He was looking worried.

'Many of my people are in Route 6 now. They have stopped the prisoners from taking the drugs. They are no longer under alien control. They are waiting for us to attack,' Jane looked at Matt. 'My plan will work if we have someone from The Firm on our side. Someone who has fought an alien already,' she said.

Matt smiled. 'I knew working for them would come in handy one day.'

Jane laughed. She squeezed his hand. 'Your moment has come, Matt. You can make things right.'

Jane kissed Matt on the cheek. Matt blushed.

'With the leader of The Enemy here, we can't lose!' joked Matt. He looked at Sam. Sam still looked worried.

'What am I going to do?' he said. 'Hide until it's over, then make us a cup of coffee?'

'You wanted to know what I did at work, Sam,' said Matt. 'Now it's time for you to find out. We're going to fight for our freedom. We're going to win.'

QUIZ

1. Why couldn't Sam make Matt a coffee?

2. Who rescued Matt and Sam from the fire?

3. Why didn't they stay with Jane's friends for long?

4. What were the aliens building?

5. Why did the aliens want to create a new ice age?

6. Why did Matt allow himself to kill for The Firm?

7. What name did The Firm give to humans that were fighting for freedom?

8. Why did Jane, Matt and Sam need to go to Route 6?

9. Why did Jane think Matt would help her plan to work?

10. Why did Matt blush?

GLOSSARY

dangerous — likely to cause harm or problems

drugged — taking tablets that stop you having free will

freedom — being able to think or act freely

prisoner — someone who is held against their will

shield — something that acts as a barrier

shiver — shaking with cold

survivors — people who remain alive after an accident or dangerous event

under enemy control — being told what to do by aliens

ANSWERS

1. Sam's cafe had been burnt down

2. Jane

3. The Firm arrived and started asking questions about them

4. A shield

5. They could only live in the cold and dark

6. He was drugged

7. The Enemy

8. To stop the main computer powering the shield

9. He knew how The Firm worked and had already fought an alien

10. Jane kissed him

CASE FILE

AUTHOR NAME
Paul Blum

JOB
Teacher

LAST KNOWN LOCATION
London, England

NOTES
Before The Crash taught in London schools. Author of *The Extraordinary Files* and *Shadows*. Believed to be in hiding from The Firm. Wanted for questioning. Seems to know more about the new ice age than he should ...